ULTIMAT

2ND EDITION

Everything a teacher needs to
know to implement RTI

Pat Quinn

---

*The nation's leading trainer of teachers in
the RTI implementation process shares the
wisdom gained through thousands of
successful implementations
of Response to Intervention*

Ultimate RTI
Second Edition

Pat Quinn

ISBN: 978-0-615-40801-9
Copyright© 2010

Printed in the United States of America

Table of Contents

Introduction...

Thank you for joining me on this journey into the world of Response to Intervention.

RTI can be confusing, complex and intimidating...but it does not need to be.

I remember the first time I heard about Response to Intervention. Eager to grasp the concept, I went out and bought three books on the topic and read them over a single weekend. When I finished reading the books, I still had no idea what RTI was or what I was supposed to do differently to apply it in my classroom.

That is the problem with most books, articles, papers and training regarding RTI. It speaks only systematically and theoretically about how it is supposed to look on a global scale. If that is the type of view you are looking for, you have definitely purchased the wrong book.

I take a completely different approach. I start with the question, "As a teacher, what does this look like in my classroom?"

From the beginning, I have looked at RTI as a process that will only succeed if regular classroom teachers buy into the process. That's why I attempted to provide information in this book to be concrete, practical, and easy to apply to your situation.

This book consists of two sections. The first half of the book contains answers to the toughest questions teachers have about implementing RTI. The second half of the book contains over 100 examples of what RTI looks like in real classrooms and real schools around the country.

About the Author...
Why Me?

So, what makes me qualified to write the *Ultimate Guide for Teachers* on a topic as vast and complicated as Response to Intervention?

If you wonder about that also, don't worry; I wouldn't be my first choice, either!

I looked all over for a practical book for teachers on the topic. What I found was a set of books that often failed to recognize that a typical classroom teacher has 35 students who have diverse abilities. They have no paraprofessionals sitting around waiting to help and no parent volunteers who are qualified to deliver interventions or monitor student progress. They do not have big budgets, extra time, or a desire to sit in high-level planning meetings for two years planning something that will go away as fast as the last trend that came down the river.

I wondered if I was the only one struggling with the lack of mentorship and sources to bring RTI to fruition. Did anyone share the challenges I encountered? To find the answers to those questions, I started a little newsletter for people looking for practical solutions to implementing Response to Intervention.

In a very short time, I received a very strong message:

I was not alone.

Today, over 4,000 teachers subscribe to my RTI newsletter, making it the largest circulated newsletter on the topic in the world. If you do not subscribe to the newsletter yet, sign up today at:

www.TotalRTI.com

As the author of this newsletter, I receive questions, ideas, strategies, tips and techniques every day from teachers implementing RTI in their schools. The purpose of this book is to share those ideas and strategies with you. I answer dozens of questions about RTI every week—so I have learned the common stumbling blocks that you might run into at your school. I also have included over 100 examples of what teachers are doing to make this process work at their schools.

I hope this book answers your questions. If it doesn't, let me know! If it does, I'd also like to hear from you. You can send your questions, comments, strategies and techniques to me at any time:

pat@betterteachingonline.com

Thanks for reading the book and good luck!

~ Pat Quinn~
"The RTI Guy"
www.TotalRTI.com

A Word about Tiers...

Across the country, states have adopted slightly different models of RTI. Some of these models use Three Tiers, while others use four tiers or even five.

For the purpose of clarity, this book will consistently use a three tier model. In most of my answers, I have tried to stay consistent and refer to the following tiers:

- Tier One – Full class instruction and full class interventions

- Tier Two – Small group interventions done with groups of five or fewer students

- Tier Three – Special services, often delivered by a special education teacher in a small group or one-on-one

If your state is using a model with more than three tiers, I know you will be able to "translate" the information to your model.

SECTION ONE

A SIMPLE EXPLANATION OF RESPONSE TO INTERVENTION

Response to Intervention:
A Simple Explanation

I begin this book with a simple explanation of Response to Intervention for two reasons. First, to establish a common language between us so that when we refer to certain words we are certain of our meaning.

The second, and the most important, reason is to model for you how simple RTI can really become.

The biggest mistake that schools make as they implement Response to Intervention is in the way they introduce and first explain RTI to the regular classroom teachers.

Response to Intervention cannot be something that the Special Education Department is doing. If RTI is something that the Special Education Department is doing at your school, your school is not really doing RTI.

Your school is not really doing RTI until your regular classroom teachers fully embrace and fully participate.

If the first time you explain RTI to your teachers, you explain it as something big and complicated, they will simply not participate.

On the other hand, if the first time your explain RTI to your teachers, you explain it as something simple and familiar, they will fully embrace and fully participate. That's how you will know that you are really doing RTI at your school!

So, let us begin with a simple explanation of Response to Intervention.

WHAT IS RTI?

RTI is a process of helping struggling students become successful. The process focuses on how a specific student responds to a specific intervention. In its simplest form, RTI includes the following steps:

- ✓ Identify a struggling student
- ✓ Implement an intervention to solve the problem
- ✓ Check to see if it worked

If the intervention works, you should naturally continue it. If the intervention does not work, you should try a different intervention.

THE BASIC STEPS
OF THE RTI PROCESS

RTI does not have to be as complicated as some people make it. I am amazed that I can read an entire book on RTI and still not have any idea what RTI is or how I would go about implementing it in my classroom.

Every implementation of RTI includes basic steps:

Universal Screening:

Identify students who are behind or struggling. For behavioral purposes, this often means looking over your data such as attendance, etc., to identify struggling or potentially struggling students.

Tier One: Full-Class Instruction:

Use a scientifically validated method to teach your full class. Every teacher that I know teaches their class about behavior. If you have not read any of Harry Wong's books, you should go get one and read it to learn about the importance of this process early in the school year.

Fidelity Check of Full-Class Intervention:

Have another person observe the teaching to make sure it is being done correctly.

Progress Monitoring During Full-Class Intervention:

Measure the progress of the students identified as struggling in the Universal Screening process. Progress monitoring for behavior is observational data, counting the number of occurrences of a specific behavior. If you are working on a student staying in their desk, count how many times they leave their desk in a certain period of time. If you are working on timeliness, count how many days each week they come to class on time.

Decision Time!

If after six weeks of receiving your full-class instruction your data shows that the student is not improving, you need to do more. For these specific students, you should move on to a Tier Two intervention.

Tier Two: Small Group Intervention:

Implement a different intervention for the small group of students who are not making progress with the full-class intervention. The group of students should share the same problem, and the intervention should be instructional in nature. Always remember: Interventions always involve instruction. Detentions, suspensions and other punishments are not interventions. Candy, games, and other rewards are not interventions. Interventions are when someone sits with a student and teaches them new skills and behaviors.

Fidelity Check of Small Group Intervention:

Have another person observe the small group intervention to make sure it is being taught correctly.

Progress Monitoring During Small Group Intervention:

Measure the progress of students who are receiving the small group intervention. Just like Tier One progress monitoring, this is observational data, counting the specific behavior you are trying to change.

Decision Time, Again!

After six weeks of receiving small group instruction, you should have enough data to determine if the intervention is effective or not. If your data shows that the student is not improving, STOP the intervention—it is not working. You probably do not have the time or money to waste on an intervention that is not working. Instead, you should try something else and measure to see if that works. If the intervention is causing improvement, continue the intervention until the students achieves an acceptable level of behavior.

Next Tiers...

At this point, schools in different states take different approaches. Some schools will try Tier Two again, with a different (more intense) intervention. Other schools go to what they call Tier Three, which is a different (more intense) intervention. Eventually, you will either find an intervention that is effective to change the behavior, or you will need to move to an eligibility meeting to discuss special education services.

This concludes the simple explanation of Response to Intervention.

As you can see, it does not need to be big or complicated. It does not need to be new or scary.

It is my experience that if you keep it simple for your teachers, they will fully participate in this process. Having the full participation of regular classroom teachers is essential for successful implementation of Response to Intervention.

Let us now take a close look at some of the key steps in this simple process.

<u>Universal Screening</u>

The first step of the RTI process is a Universal Screening.

Purpose: The only purpose of a Universal Screener is to identify which students you want to monitor more closely during Tier 1.

The purpose of a Universal Screener is not to place students in groups. As a matter of fact, by definition, RTI does not use the results of a static test to place students in groups. Instead, RTI looks at a student's response to instruction over time to make decisions.

So, don't over think your Universal Screener and don't overspend. It only has one purpose: to identify which students you want to monitor more closely during Tier 1. We will use progress monitoring from that point on to make our important decisions.

Choosing an Elementary Universal Screener:

It is not a good idea to look for one universal screening tool across grades K-5. The students have different needs at different grades.

In grades K-2, I would recommend an oral reading fluency test as your universal screener. DIBELS is the most popular one in the country, but there are plenty of others.

In grades 3-5, I recommend a reading comprehension test as your universal screener. The STAR reading test from Renaissance Learning is a great example, but there are plenty of others.

Both of these tests will give you the data you need. Both are appropriate for the ages mentioned. I don't see a benefit of using one tool for all grades K-5, and it often forces you to give age-inappropriate assessments.

Universal Screening at the Middle School and High School Level:

Many middle schools and high schools do not use a distinct Universal Screening tool. If you keep in mind that the only purpose of a Universal Screener is to identify which students you will monitor more closely during Tier One, you understand why this is the case.

By the time a student reaches 7th or 8th grade, we certainly do not lack performance data. We have years of standardized testing scores and years of grades and teacher feedback. This data can be examined to choose which students you want to monitor more closed during Tier One.

For instance, but the time a student reaches middle school or high school, you should already know their reading comprehension level. You don't need to spend time giving a separate test to ascertain that information. If you don't already know it, I would administer a test such as the STAR Reading Test from Renaissance Learning.

Tier One Full-Class Instruction and Fidelity Check:

Successful RTI schools always have a keen eye on what is going on in the classroom. Although book after book is written about small group interventions and tiered interventions, everything begins with classroom instruction. Make sure your school has done everything it can to improve the quality of instruction that every student receives every day. This is your first line of defense...make sure it is a strong one!

A fidelity check will not only ensure that teachers are teaching with the best method, but also will document the evidence based on practices and materials being used.

Progress Monitoring

Progress Monitoring is monitoring the progress of _certain students_ in a _specific skill_ _over time_.

As you can see, there are three major parts:

1. Monitor the progress of certain students
2. Monitor progress in a specific skill
3. Monitor progress over time

Let's look at each of the parts separately:

Monitor the progress of certain students.

Do you need to monitor the progress of all of your students in class? No. Who do you monitor? Only the students identified with your Universal Screening tool. (That was the purpose of the Universal Screener.)

Sometimes, teachers get overwhelmed about the thought of monitoring the progress of every student. You do not need to do this. Only monitor the progress of the few students identified with the Universal Screening tool. So, in a typical class there may be three or four students who you should be monitoring.

Monitor progress in a specific skill.

This is the hardest part of progress monitoring for teachers to understand.

If you ask most teachers whether or not they monitor progress, they will respond, "Yes. I give the chapter one test, I give the chapter two test, and I give the chapter three test."

The chapter one test, the chapter two test, and the chapter three test are not progress monitoring in an RTI context. This is because the chapter one test, the chapter two test, and the chapter three test are measuring three different sets of skills.

You need to measure the SAME SKILL each time. Not the same test items, but test items at the same level, measuring the same skill.

Monitor progress over time.

The progress of a particular student needs to be monitored repeatedly over time. Most experts would say to measure the progress 10 to 12 times over at least six weeks of instruction.

Each time you measure the progress, you will get a score. You should graph the scores on a simple graph with dates on the bottom and scores going up the left side. The graph may look like this:

When you graph 12 scores on this graph, you can connect the points with a line. The line will either travel up, down, or straight across. The direction of this line will tell you whether or not your instruction is working with a particular student.

If the instruction is working, keep doing it.

If the instruction is not working, do something more.

This is where the term "Response to Intervention" actually comes from. We are measuring and graphing the student's _response_ to the _intervention_.

Progress Monitoring Tests and Tools

At the youngest grade levels, progress monitoring in the area of Reading is usually done with an oral reading fluency test. Oral

Reading Fluency is certainly a good measure of reading progress, and it is preferred by many teachers. The reason for this is that Oral Reading Fluency is correlated with just about any indicator of good reading, and it takes just a few minutes to assess.

As students get older, schools often switch to a test of reading comprehension level. This type of test will give the students' comprehension levels as a grade level (such as 4.2) or a score (such as 400).

In the area of Mathematics, students are usually given a test of basic math facts at the youngest grade levels. Because this is fast and easy to measure, teachers will often perform this type of test with the entire class, even though you only need to monitor the progress of a few specific students.

As students get older, they are often given a basic math pre-test, measuring their proficiency in certain essential skills.

Secondary Progress Monitoring

Teachers who teach subjects other than Math and Reading and teachers who teach at secondary grade levels often have a difficult time picturing what progress monitoring might look like in their classrooms. Teachers at these grade levels often have more focus on the "topic of the day" than they do on "big picture" skills and ideas. As teachers, we cannot slow down from the pacing guide or the "topic of the day," lest we fall behind and do not complete enough instruction before standardized testing or the end of the school year.

To create effective progress monitoring in these classes, we ask teachers to think about the "essential skills" that are bigger than the "topic of the day." What are the big skills that students acquire in your class? These "essential skills" are bigger than any day, any chapter, or even one course. They cut across your entire curriculum.

Schools should spend professional development time meeting by department to determine these "essential skills." After an essential skill is developed, the teachers should develop a way to measure student progress in this area.

For example, a group of science teachers met and identified "Graphing" as an essential skill. It was used in every chapter of every course they taught. They developed a simple rubric to measure a student's proficiency at graphing.

Now they have a tool that can be used to measure a student's progress from the first day of school in this area. Certain students (those identified with a Universal Screening Tool) will have their graphing progress measured and graphed repeatedly throughout the school year. Classroom instruction will work for many of these students, and their scores will improve. Other students will need additional Tier Two support to improve in the area of graphing.

Every subject and every grade level can do this, but it requires stepping back from the "Topic of the Day" and focusing instead on "Essential Skills."

Developing a System of Progress Monitoring

Progress Monitoring is new for most teachers. It should not be assumed that most teachers know how to do it or are comfortable with it. We were not trained on it in college and have not been doing it for years.

One of the essential components of your school successfully implementing RTI will be professional development on Progress Monitoring.

Here are signs that your school is making progress:

Elementary:

- The school selects and purchases a tool to measure progress in Reading and Math.

- Teachers are trained in the use of this tool and are comfortable graphing the results.

- Teachers routinely show up to meetings with graphs of student progress data.

Secondary:

- Professional Development time is spent at the secondary level so teachers can identify "Essential Skills" and develop tools to measure them.

- Teachers use the developed tool to measure the progress of certain students.

- Teachers routinely show up to meetings with graphs of student progress data.

Progress monitoring is at the very core of RTI, because it is the only way we can measure the student's _response_ to the _intervention_.

Tier Two:
Small Group Interventions

Schools often struggle to implement small group interventions because they feel they lack time and resources. There are eight different models of implementing small group interventions. Each of the models has its own strengths and weaknesses.

The first three models implement small group interventions, instead of core instruction. This means that the intervention takes place during the same time that core instruction is happening in the classroom. Some will argue that this is not an effective system because there are no additional minutes of instruction given. Others will assert that having a smaller student-to-adult ratio and more targeted instruction carries many benefits compared to less individualized large-class instruction.

The last five models implement small group interventions, in addition to core instruction. This means that the student stays in the classroom for all of core instruction. Then, at another time of the day, the student receives additional minutes of instruction. This seems like a more effective solution, but the logistics of implementing such a system cause many schools to give up this effort.

A school should choose a model from the list below to implement.

```
MODEL 1:
Classroom Teacher Delivers
Intervention During Class
```

In this model, the student receives a targeted intervention delivered by the classroom teacher during actual class time. The teacher needs to juggle teaching both the full class and the small group of students receiving the targeted intervention.

Strengths: This model is easy for one teacher to implement on their own. It does not take the cooperation of anyone else in the school. Continuity of instruction is maintained because the teacher does all of the planning and instruction.

Weaknesses: Almost impossible for most teachers to pull off. It is extremely difficult to lead both your full class and a targeted small group effectively at the same time.

```
MODEL 2:
Another Adult Delivers Intervention
During Class in the Classroom
```

In this model, another adult comes into the classroom and delivers a targeted intervention to a small group of students during class time. The adult delivering the intervention may be a reading specialist, an instructional aide, or any other adult trained to deliver the intervention.

Strengths: This model is easy to schedule, and it removes the burden of leading the small group intervention from the classroom teacher.

Weaknesses: Sometimes the noise from the small group will distract the class, and sometimes the noise from the class will distract the small group.

> **MODEL 3:**
> Another Adult Delivers Intervention
> During Class Outside of the Classroom

This model is similar to Model 2, but the intervention is delivered in a location other than the regular classroom.

Strengths: The small group meets in a quiet, secluded location to maximize concentration and focus.

Weaknesses: Extra space is needed.

> **MODEL 4:**
> Classroom Teacher Delivers
> Intervention Outside of Class Time

In this model, the student remains in class for core instruction. At another time during the day, the teacher meets with the student to deliver additional minutes of targeted instruction.

Strengths: More minutes of instruction. Continuity of instruction.

Weaknesses: The teacher only has so many minutes during the day, so this usually steals from planning time. The student may not have free time and may need to miss a different class to receive this instruction.

> **MODEL 5:**
> Another Adult Delivers Intervention
> Outside of Class Time

This model is similar to Model 4, except the targeted intervention is delivered by an adult other than the regular classroom teacher. The adult delivering the intervention may be a reading specialist, an instructional aide, or any other adult trained to deliver the intervention.

Strengths: Easier to schedule. Less burden on the classroom teacher.

Weaknesses: Requires good communication between the classroom teacher and the adult delivering the intervention. Student may still be missing another class.

> **MODEL 6:**
> Common Location

In this model, teachers of a particular subject work together to create a location where students can go for additional instruction. For instance, math teachers may form a math lab where students can go throughout the day to receive extra math help. Certain students are assigned to go this location at a specific time for a targeted small group intervention. Reading and writing teachers may form a similar skills lab.

Strengths: This is a great model for secondary schools which have students moving around the building throughout the day.

Weaknesses: Continuity of instruction is difficult because different teachers provide help in this location throughout the day.

MODEL 7:
Flex Time

In the model, the school builds into its schedule a 20 or 30 minute block specifically for interventions. At this time, the entire school stops its regular schedule. Students who are not in intervention groups go to the gym, the cafeteria, or a study hall and are supervised. Every teacher in the school leads a small group intervention.

Strengths: Intervention time is not stolen from other classes. Each teacher only leads one small group.

Weaknesses: Students who need help in more than one area may have trouble receiving it.

MODEL 8:
Flooding

This model is similar to Model 7, but instead of the entire school having "intervention time" at the same time, individual grade levels take turns having "intervention time." During this time, the grade level is "flooded" with additional personnel.

Let's look at an example:

At a school that I visited recently, the first grade classrooms went into intervention time from 9:00 to 9:30 a.m. During this time, seven additional adults moved into that area to lead groups. Who were the adults? One counselor, one reading specialist, on administrator, one special education teacher, two instructional aides, and one parent volunteer.

These seven adults joined the two classroom teachers to form NINE separate small groups. There were a total of 53 students in the two first grade classes, making the average group size six students. (Of course, some of the more advanced groups were larger, and some students with more intense needs were in much smaller groups...but the average size was six.)

Students worked in these small groups for 30 minutes on intense reading interventions targeted to their specific needs. Progress monitoring was done weekly. Groups were juggled and re-formed every six weeks based on student growth and progress.

At 9:30 a.m., the "flood" of adults moved on to second grade, and from 9:40 to 10:10, those classes went into "intervention time."

"The Flood" worked their way through the grade levels throughout the day.

This example had ALL students in small groups. Other schools leave 25 of the most advanced students in a large class setting with one of the classroom teachers and just have some of the students (those who are struggling) go into groups. This would either make your groups smaller or lower the number of extra adults necessary to implement this model.

Remember: You do not need to implement this at all grade levels. As a matter of fact, schools that have successfully implemented this model usually start with just one grade level (usually kindergarten or first grade) and then add one grade to the model each year. This helps the "rotating team of extra adults" adjust to their new roles over time.

Strengths: Usually can be implemented with existing personnel.

Weaknesses: Staff needs to be trained to take on new roles. Some staff members may not want to transition to new roles.

Getting Started

Four areas to focus on as you begin implementing Response to Intervention:

First, you should think about "Outstanding Classroom Instruction."

Are your classroom teachers doing everything they can to individualize and differentiate instruction? You may need to work on improving classroom instruction before moving on to the rest of RTI.

Second, you should think about "Professional Development that is Well-Planned and Well-Executed."

Professional development is HUGE when you are implementing RTI. From understanding what RTI is to learning about screening, interventions, and progress monitoring, there is a lot to learn! Make sure your school has a plan in place to deliver this material to your teachers in an orderly and meaningful way. Also, PLEASE make sure that your professional development is delivered by someone who has experience teaching at the grade level that your teachers teach. At the secondary level (after an introductory presentation), I think the professional development should also be delivered in subject-area groups...not all departments together.

The next item to consider is, "Are your teachers making graphs?"

This one separates the pretenders from the contenders. If your school is really doing RTI, then your teachers are doing progress monitoring. If your teachers are doing progress monitoring, then they should be graphing the results over time.

Simple Steps:

1. Choose an essential skill.

2. Find a way to measure that skill.

3. Measure certain students repeated over time in that skill.

4. Graph the results.

Many people will recommend software programs to graph the data. I prefer a clipboard and a pencil. Whatever you do...make sure your teachers know how to measure and graph student progress!

Finally, you should think about "Having Interventions in Key Areas."

If you want RTI to fail at your school, leave the burden of finding good interventions with a teacher and give them no time or resources to find and purchase them. On the other hand, if you would like RTI to really happen, you should equip your teachers with a solid Tier 2 small group intervention in each key area, starting with Reading, Math, and Behavior, then moving on to other key subject areas at your school.

These four areas are essential to effective RTI implementation — you will find them present in every school that is successfully doing Response to Intervention. Check back often over this list of four imperatives to make sure your school is headed in the right direction!

SECTION TWO

YOUR TOUGHEST QUESTIONS ANSWERED

About RTI

 What is RTI?

RTI is a process of helping struggling students become successful. The process focuses on how a specific student responds to a specific intervention. In its simplest form, RTI includes the following steps:

- Identify a struggling student
- Implement an intervention to solve the problem
- Check to see if it worked

If the intervention works, you should naturally continue it. If the intervention does not work, you should try a different intervention.

The belief behind RTI is that being "behind" does not indicate that a student has a learning disability. A learning disability is applicable when a student does not "respond" to a scientifically validated intervention like other students.

What are the basic steps of the RTI process?

RTI does not have to be as complicated as some people make it out to be. I am amazed that I can read an entire book on RTI and still not have any idea what RTI is or how I would go about implementing it in my classroom.

To save you from doing the same type of research and still not receiving the information you need, I've simplified and defined RTI. I hope it provides you with a greater understanding and a broader feel for what RTI is and how you can effectively use it in your classroom.

Every implementation of RTI includes basic steps:

Universal Screening
Measure all students to identify students who are behind.

Tier One: Full-Class Intervention
Use a scientifically validated method to teach your full class.

Fidelity Check of Full-Class Intervention
Have another person observe the teaching to make sure it is being done correctly.

Progress Monitoring during Full-Class Intervention
Measure the progress of the students identified as behind in the Universal Screening.

Tier Two: Small Group Intervention

Implement a different intervention for the small group of students who are not making progress with the full class intervention.

Fidelity Check of Small Group Intervention

Have another person observe the small group intervention to make sure it is being taught correctly.

Progress Monitoring During Small Group Intervention

Measure the progress of students who are receiving the small group intervention.

Tier Three: Special Services

At this point, schools take different approaches. Many schools will now move to providing specialized services from special education staff to those students are not responding.

 Does our school have to be implementing Professional Learning Communities (PLCs) for RTI to work?

The answer is no—you do not have to have Professional Learning Communities in place, BUT you also should not be working alone.

RTI is not designed to be implemented individually. Team is at the very heart of RTI Professional Learning Communities are one form of that team.

From the earliest identification of students using universal screenings all the way through to the final eligibility decision, every step of the process is meant to be worked on as a team.

When RTI is thrust into a teacher's lap, they feel helpless and overwhelmed. THEY SHOULD! RTI is not the responsibility of the teacher, or ANY ONE INDIVIDUAL, for that matter. It is the responsibility of the team.

Now, that being said, every team member has a role to play. The teacher does have specific responsibilities, as do all other members of the team.

To avoid overwhelm, teachers should know that they are not expected to do the following:

- Select a Universal Screening without assistance from other staff members

- Check the fidelity of their own Tier One Intervention

- Choose a small group intensive intervention without consulting with other staff members

- Be the only observer of the student's response to any intervention

- Make a decision about whether an intensive intervention was successful

All of these tasks, plus many others, should be done in close consultation with other staff members—so SURROUND YOUR TEACHERS WITH EITHER A PLC OR ANOTHER TEAM!

Here are two things you probably did not know:

> You should surround your *most resistant* teachers with your *best* team members. This seems to fly in the face of logic - but it works.

> When teachers are hesitant to work with the team, it is usually not because they don't need their assistance or won't benefit from working with them. It is usually because they are afraid that they themselves do not know enough or have enough interventions. It is this very LACK OF CONFIDENCE that makes them hesitant to work with a team. Address this fear with help and training, not threats or ignoring.

Every school has some teachers who are hesitant or resistant to try RTI. My experience is that this can be overcome with help from a supportive team, whether or not this is in the form of a Professional Learning Community.

 RTI seems to have so many steps. Is one step more important than the others?

The answer is: interventions. The whole process relies on having good interventions.

You can do every other part of RTI perfectly, and if you don't have good interventions, it just won't work.

Your first hours as a staff, as a team, or as an individual starting RTI should be spent examining the interventions you currently have and finding new ones.

Look specifically at the most common and most debilitating deficiencies your students have and choose the best research-validated interventions to address them. Specificity is key—choose specific interventions to address very specific problems.
Use good up-to-date resources like the What Works Clearinghouse (www.w-w-c.org) to check the research validation of your chosen interventions. Also, check with other teachers using the intervention to make sure it will work in your unique situation.

After you have good interventions, the screening, monitoring, recording and decision-making will all fall into place...but it all starts with an intervention that works.

The process can be big and scary—but don't let it be that way. Start with interventions.

Implementation
of RTI

 What is the first step a teacher should take as they begin to implement RTI in their school or classroom?

Believe it or not, every person in your school will not be excited that you'll be implementing RTI. Resistance to different interventions being used with different students is not unusual. It is a symptom of a common problem: Failure to create a culture of individual differences in your classroom and school.

The first step we need to take as we begin to implement RTI in any school or classroom is to create a culture where individual differences are recognized and celebrated. Every student should know their unique characteristics and be tolerant of others. Students should be comfortable doing one activity in the classroom while other students are working on a different activity. Students should be comfortable with differentiated instruction being used daily in the classroom.

Without this foundation, your efforts to implement RTI will be fruitless. Response to Intervention requires that certain interventions be used with some students, but not others. I have seen far too many classrooms where the students (and their parents) resist this because the teacher has not created a culture of individual differences.

What are the first steps school administration should take as the school begins to implement RTI?

There are two steps that any administration serious about implementing RTI must take. The first is to train the staff. The second is to reallocate staff time.

Each particular group of staff members needs to have time reallocated. Teachers will need extra time to choose scientifically validated interventions and to do progress monitoring of students.

Certain other staff members and specialists need to take the time they used to spend testing students in a discrepancy model and reallocate it to check fidelity and observe students in an RTI model. Paraprofessionals also need their time reallocated so they can assist teachers in progress monitoring and small group interventions.

All groups need adequate time to be trained in the selection, implementation, and monitoring of scientifically validated interventions. Failure to reallocate sufficient time for these activities is a recipe for partial ineffective implementation of RTI. Too many schools love the idea of RTI, but they do not reallocate the time necessary for proper training and implementation.

Is RTI appropriate for middle school and high school?

The answer is a resounding "YES"! In states that are ahead of the curve with RTI, such as Illinois, the majority of my activities are devoted to helping middle schools and high schools. Often, districts will focus all of their early efforts on the elementary level, leaving the middle and high schools to follow later.

There are specific steps that teachers are taking at the secondary school level to help students and implement RTI. Let's look separately at what schools are doing in Reading, Math, and General Study and Organizational Skills.

READING

As No Child Left Behind ratchets up the pressure, high schools around the country are doing everything they can to help readers achieve grade level proficiency.

Because the student's traditional courses are already packed with content, teachers are hesitant (or unable because of the wide span of abilities) to provide targeted reading instruction because it would require them to sacrifice other content which they are also required to cover.

For this reason, schools are taking students who are reading well below grade level (or not reading at all) and providing them with additional reading instruction during another part of their day. Depending on the individual's schedule, this additional instruction may happen before school, during study hall or lunch, immediately after school or in the evening.

This instruction is most effective if it is individualized and self-paced. Schools use reading specialists, teachers, paraprofessionals and computer-aided instruction to provide this extra support.

Oftentimes, students must sacrifice taking an elective class (or delay taking a specific class) to make room for this extra instruction. Schools should not regret requiring a student to do this because they know the additional reading instruction will help the student in every aspect of their academics.

MATH

Traditionally, math classes are a bit more ability-grouped at the high school level, with students taking algebra, geometry, or pre-algebra.

When students are not yet ready for algebra at the high school level, schools are increasingly finding it ineffective to continue teaching a traditional pre-algebra class. There are many reasons why this is ineffective, including the fact that this mode of instruction has been shown to be less effective for this particular group of students.

Instead, what many schools are developing is an individualized, self-paced curriculum that focuses specifically on the student's deficiencies which contribute toward his or her lack of success in algebra.

If you have 25 ninth-grade students who lack the prerequisite skills to take algebra, my guess is that each of them is lacking a different set of skills. Some may be missing fractions. Some may be missing negatives. Some may be missing exponents. Yet, there are some who may be missing all of the above.

Given that they are all lacking different skills, why would we put them all through the same remediation?

The student who lacks only fraction skills should focus on fractions. The student who laces only positive/negative skills should focus on negatives. You get the idea.

So, instead of taking classrooms full of students and walking them lock-step through a pre-algebra course, schools have taken the same group of students and individualized the instruction toward each student's deficits.

Using a pre-test to measure what skills they lack, an individual course of study is designed to help them be ready for algebra. Using this method, most schools find they can prepare a student to be ready for algebra in one semester, rather than one year. (Of course, your schedule may not allow students to begin algebra in January, but that is another matter.)

Some schools deliver the individualized instruction through computer-aided instruction with great programs, such as Skillstutor. For more information, visit www.skillstutor.com.

Other schools have "modularized" their pre-algebra curriculum into packets or "modules" so that students can focus solely on the areas where they need the most help, with the teacher delivering one-on-one or small-group help when needed.

In the end, you will see these results:

- Students will be prepared for algebra faster because they won't be sitting through instruction on topics they already understand.

- Behavior problems go down, because students are not bored in a self-paced curriculum.

- Effort and attendance go up because the amount of time the student spends in the class is directly related to how hard they work and the competency level they show.

- Success in algebra goes up because students need to show competency in all areas before taking the class. (Under the old method, getting great grades in some chapters of pre-algebra could mask incompetence in other areas.)

- Graduation and college enrollment rates go up when you have a program that helps students pass algebra.

Now, that's not a bad target to shoot for, if you ask me!

GENERAL STUDY AND ORGANIZATIONAL SKILLS

In a more general sense, there are also many schools implementing Tier 1 and Tier 2 interventions focusing on cross-curricular skills, such as organization and motivation.

45

Schools all over the country are flocking to Vicki Phillip's "Personal Development" curriculum for its wealth of student activities research proven to increase student self-esteem, organizational skills, goal-setting and learning. Check it out at www.personaldevelopment.org

Even with tightly packed schedules, teachers are finding the time to implement specific classroom wide and small-group interventions, because they know that time spent on these foundational skills will pay off for years to come.

Don't let anyone fool you into thinking that helping students with essential organizational, note-taking, memorization and time management skills is outside your curriculum. It is not. It is this very set of skills that your curriculum was originally developed to enhance and develop.

 What should Staff Development look like in a school that is starting to implement RTI?

Professional Development is the most important component of a successful RTI implementation. It must be well-planned and well-executed.

Some facts you should know:

FACT: RTI training cannot be done in one day. It is a process of trying new techniques that takes time.

FACT: RTI training will look different for different teachers. An elementary teacher working with struggling readers needs different training than a middle school art teacher with misbehaving students.

FACT: RTI training must include resources for staff members to find interventions and progress monitoring tools.

FACT: RTI training must be accountable. Staff members need to do more than LEARN about RTI. They need to TRY it. Every step of the way they should be trying the new techniques that they learn.

So, what's the plan? I recommend that you begin with an assessment of what your students' current practices are, as well as an assessment of the resources your school currently has in place. You can design this on your own or use a pre-written assessment. I use the "RTI Online Readiness Assessment" from School Perceptions.

Implementing RTI at a school does require teachers to find and use new interventions—but even if your school is not implementing RTI, teachers should always be on the lookout for new techniques that work.

Because teachers' plates are already so full of increased requirements and accountability, I do believe we need to make it as easy as possible for them to learn about and utilize effective interventions. Therefore, I recommend the following:

- Set aside some professional development time for the collection of strategies that are currently being used. Let grade-level teams (at the elementary level) and subject-area teams (at the secondary level) come up with one or two "Best Practice" interventions to use for each specific deficiency they commonly encounter.

- When doing this activity, they will undoubtedly expose gaps: common student deficiencies encountered which lack an effective intervention. Encourage them to work together, along with district level (or regional educational service agency level, if possible) specialists, to research and acquire interventions in this area. You will need to set aside professional development time or create extra "curriculum writing" paid time for this, or it will never happen.

- Create a "common repository" where interventions are documented and resources are kept. At a school, this might be in the office or work room. At the district, this might be in the curriculum director's space. Most schools using a shared computer network or intranet will make this a "virtual repository" with folders for each subject area, grade level and deficiency.

When teachers begin implementing RTI, they do not need to be bombarded with dozens of new interventions. Instead, they need one or two interventions that really work for the problems they commonly deal with, and they need a place that they can go to get interventions for new problems.

Where do we find the time to implement RTI?

There is no doubt that RTI will take time. The question is: Where do we get this time? Let's go through the process step by step, beginning with Universal Screening.

UNIVERSAL SCREENING

Most schools should already be doing some sort of Universal Screening so that teachers know the skill levels and specific deficiencies of their students. This does not need to be an add-on...try to use a screening that is already in place.

TIER ONE

Tier One interventions are delivered to the full class. Again, this requires no extra work and takes no more time than your regular teaching. It is just an assurance that you are using a research-validated curriculum or intervention with your class.

PROGRESS MONITORING
DURING TIER ONE

Progress monitoring during Tier One is an extra task - probably something that you were not doing with a specific subset of students prior to RTI. You can do the progress monitoring with your full class in certain areas (such as basic math facts) or you can individually measure and record a select small group of students. Some schools have select paraprofessionals or specialists who help with this. If your school doesn't, however, keep reading to find ways to create this time with small groups.

TIER TWO

Now, it's time for the big question:

 How do you implement Tier 2 small group interventions while still teaching the rest of your class?

First, you need to decide if your Tier 2 interventions are going to be "instead of" the large class instruction or "in addition to" large class instruction. Either is okay, but you should know that the method you pick will determine how the intervention is implemented.

Options from other schools:

> ➤ Some schools implement the Tier 2 small group interventions during class. The teacher creates "centers" or "learning stations" around the classroom. The students rotate among the centers in small groups. A teacher sits at the table of one of those stations, which is where the intervention is implemented.

> ➤ Some schools use extra personnel, such as instructional aides or reading specialists, to carry out the small group interventions. I was never at a school lucky enough to have this advantage, but I was just at a school in Ohio

where an aide spent her whole day pulling small groups out of classes and doing interventions.

➤ Other schools use a paraprofessional to supervise the classroom while a teacher delivers the intervention to small groups. I would hesitate to use this method too often—as the whole class deserves to have the instruction of their teacher...but many schools tell me this works for them.

➤ At some schools, two third-grade teachers will combine their classes and efforts. While one of them takes both classes and teaches them social studies, the other teacher works with small groups of students on interventions. (Note here: the interventions do not need to be about Social Studies. They are stealing from one subject to give to reading or math.) This is a great method. Think about it: if you pair up with another teacher, one of you is probably better with large group instruction and one of you is probably better with small group interventions. This method allows you to use these strengths.

➤ At other schools, the first 30 minutes of the day and/or the last 30 minutes of the day are "flex time" where students work in different groups. The small group interventions are delivered daily during this time.

➤ If your school has a study hall or extra time at lunch, it can be staffed by instructors, teachers (in lieu of supervision elsewhere), paraprofessionals, specialists or special education staff who deliver interventions to small groups of students.

> ➢ In some schools, when the rest of the class leaves to go to another teacher for classes such as art, music or physical education, a small group of students stays with the teacher and are released after they have had their intervention done or progress monitored.

Some of these methods infringe upon a teacher's planning or lunch time in order to utilize recess, student lunch, or "special" classes such as art, music or physical education when the class is with another teacher. Don't despair, though. Those aren't the only options. There are many ways for schools to implement small group interventions—and they do not all steal from the teacher's free time. Actually, if one thing gets stolen from the most, it probably is Social Studies or Science instruction. When doing so, schools are making a conscious choice that Reading or Math is a priority over other subjects.

PROGRESS MONITORING
DURING TIER TWO

Progress monitoring during Tier 2 is usually done by the same person delivering the intervention, in the same manner and at the same time that the intervention is delivered.

TIER THREE

Tier 3 Interventions (in a 3-tier model) are usually delivered by Special Education staff in much the same way that special education services were delivered before you implemented RTI.

What is Fidelity?

Fidelity is the assurance that an intervention has been delivered to the students as it was designed, and in the same manner that it was proven to be effective. There is an emphasis in RTI for an outside observer to watch the teacher deliver the intervention to assure that it was delivered correctly. "Dosage" is another term associated with Fidelity. Dosage refers to how often a student receives the intervention, and for how long each time it is delivered. You may have the best reading intervention in the world, but it will not be effective if it is given to the student once a month for five minutes. Interventions must be delivered with the correct dosage—the dosage that research proved to be effective.

Interventions and Progress Monitoring

 Where do I find all of these interventions"?

This is probably one of the most common areas where schools struggle. The search for specific interventions to solve specific problems is sometimes long and difficult, but again, this is an area that doesn't have to be as difficult as it appears.

Use the following resources and examples to help you find the perfect intervention for any situation:

Websites

We live in a world of endless information, and the internet provides us with great resources for educators to share research-validated interventions. Here are two great examples:

What Works Clearinghouse is a great resource for finding research-validated interventions. Find this website by using Google and searching for "What Works Clearinghouse."

Intervention Reviews contains thousands of reviews written by real teachers using interventions in real classrooms. You can search the database of interventions by subject area and grade level. Find this website by going to www.TotalRTI.com and clicking on the "Intervention Reviews" button.

National Organizations

There are national organizations in each discipline that offer both conferences and resources to help you locate the perfect intervention.

Two great examples:

NCTM – The National Council of Teachers of Mathematics is a great resource for Math Teachers. http://www.nctm.org/

The *International Reading Association* is dedicated to providing educators the resources needed to help every student read. http://www.reading.org/

Publishers

Because RTI has swept over the nation like a tidal wave, the major publishing companies have responded with a variety of research-validated products. If your class uses a textbook from a major publisher, there is a high likelihood that the same company has produced interventions, as well.

Two great examples:

Houghton Mifflin produces products such as *iSucceed MATH™*, a data-driven math intervention solution combining technology and print for students who have not yet mastered the fundamentals of mathematics in the early grades. www.hmco.com

Holt McDougal produces secondary products, such as *Bridges to Literature*, a transitional reading program that uses engaging literature selections, combined with strategies and skills instruction, to help less-proficient readers prepare to read on-level literature.

Researchers

Independent research organizations are actively helping us find interventions, as well. These organizations receive funding from a variety of state, regional, and national sources, but the results often will be access to interventions that help our students.

Two great examples:

The *Advanced Learning Technologies project at the University of Kansas Center for Research on Learning (ALTEC)* has created a set of heavily-used academic "skill builders" for students struggling in reading and math. They are available free at:

http://www.arcademicskillbuilders.com/

The Florida Center for Reading Research (FCRR) is loaded with specific interventions that work at different grade levels. It is the "go-to place" for many teachers. http://fcrr.org/

Private Companies

Companies around the country have jumped into the intervention game with a wide variety of products to help struggling learners. Many of these companies have been serving educators long before RTI was around and are trusted partners in schools across the nation.

Two great examples:

> *Renaissance Learning* has produced products such as *Accelerated Reader* to help schools individualize reading instruction. They also produce one of the simplest and most popular progress monitoring tools in the area of reading: the *STAR, Reading* program. Check out their RTI products at: http://www.sde.state.id.us/site/rti/resources.htm

> *Read Naturally* is quite possibly the company and product that I hear the most about. Schools and teachers that use *Read Naturally* continually rave about the success they have with specific students. http://www.readnaturally.com/

Software and Technology Companies

Software companies continue to pour out specific tools designed to help implement an intervention with a select group of students. Teachers often struggle with the Tier Two small group interventions because there is no time to work with a small group without leaving the rest of the class. Computer-aided instruction is often part of that solution.

Two great examples:

Skillstutor is an online learning system that I personally have used for years to help struggling students get the boost they need in a variety of subjects. http://www.achievementtech.com/

SRA is old enough to be a classic! But their new software and online tools are helping readers grasp key concepts and improve their reading. http://www.sraonline.com/

And that is just the start of your list of resources. Your state department of education, your district reading specialist, the teacher next door...all of these resources are available to help you find the interventions you need.

 Do Tier 2 Small Group Interventions need to be "in addition" to the instruction other students are receiving or can they be "instead of" the instruction other students are receiving?

Some teachers are implementing Tier 2 interventions, while other students are working on different work — and they are being told that a Tier 2 intervention cannot be "instead" of other instruction; it must be "in addition" to other instruction. I believe this thinking misses the point of RTI completely.

Let me explain...

Remember that the key to RTI is that the intervention is TARGETED to the specific deficiency that a student has shown. The key to Tier 2 interventions is not whether or not they are "in addition" to other instruction, it is whether or not they are "targeted" based on the deficiency that the student shows and how the student responded to the full class Tier 1 intervention.

In thousands of classrooms around the country, students are receiving their Tier 2 interventions while other students in the same room at the same time are receiving other instruction. Some of this other instruction might be targeting different deficiencies; some of it might be an extension activity for gifted and talented students, etc. That is why learning centers or learning stations are used so effectively with RTI.

Adjust your thinking a bit and try to switch from "quantity of instruction" to "targeting of instruction." You can give an "at-risk" student 300 minutes of instruction and it won't be a Tier 2 intervention because it wasn't targeted specifically to his need.

On the other hand, you can give a student the same number of minutes of instruction as all other students, but in a small group setting offer a special intervention for his problem, and measure progress during this small group instruction - and you have a Tier 2 intervention.

Of course, this doesn't work if the student is missing other essential instruction - but the idea here is that at some point you have broken the class into groups to provide instruction differentiated based on their needs.

NO! One of the areas of confusion teachers often have is the difference between an "intervention" and "progress monitoring." Even administrators and state-level people make this mistake.

Are Interventions the same thing as Progress Monitoring?

Teachers need to learn that AIMSWEB is NOT an intervention. It is a progress measuring tool that is used after an intervention.

So many times, I've asked teachers what interventions they have tried, and they answer, "AIMSWEB" or "DIBELS for reading." These are not interventions, and they definitely DO NOT increase learning, cause learning, or help students to learn. Their only purpose is to give teachers data about the effectiveness of the intervention they are using.

Interventions are instructional in nature. They are all about teaching.

Progress monitoring is testing. It is all about measuring.

My good friend, Bill, often says, "You can't make a pig heavier by measuring it!"

The same is true with your students. You don't make them smarter by simply measuring them. Students don't learn from progress monitoring. They learn from interventions.

To implement RTI, you need BOTH interventions and progress monitoring.

I am monitoring progress three times a week. Should I use the same assessment every time?

You should not use the same assessment each time, but it must be assessing the same skill and be at the same level.

If it were always an identical set of items, we could assume that student scores would go up because they would learn the individual items and become more familiar with them.

What is most important is that you are measuring the same skill at the same level. Many publishers put out sets of assessments that are on the same level. For instance, lists of words all at the same level, multiple reading passages at the same level, or multiplication problems all at the same level.

There are also multiple software programs that measure this way with randomly selected items.

 WHO can implement the interventions in RTI?

Tier 1 interventions are usually implemented by the classroom teacher and delivered to the full class.

There are no legal restrictions on who can facilitate a Tier 2 small group intervention. Some schools have the classroom teachers facilitate the intervention while the class works on other activities, or while the class is working with an Aide, another teacher (like music or Phy. Ed. class) or while the class is at lunch or recess.

Other schools have the intervention facilitated by an Aide or a Specialist, such as the reading specialist. Sometimes this is done in the classroom; sometimes it is done in a resource room or the library.

The advantage of having someone other than the teacher administer the intervention is that you can take kids from different classes into the small group.

I was at a school in Ohio where each third-grade teacher sent two kids into a resource room, where they received tier 2 intervention from an aide hired just for this purpose. After that 20-minute intervention, each fourth-grade teacher sent kids, etc.

Tier 3 interventions (in a three-tier model) are usually implemented by special education staff. These are usually very intensive interventions and often special training is needed.

A book that does a great job profiling how schools have used all of their personnel to implement RTI is *Whatever It Takes: How Professional Learning Communities Respond When Kids Don't Learn*. It is definitely worth purchasing to learn how other schools are successfully doing this.

All of the emphasis at our school seems to be on Tier Two small group interventions. Are Tier One interventions important? Shouldn't we be examining our core curriculum and instruction?

You are correct that effective implementation of RTI begins with an examination of your core curriculum. The whole pyramid collapses and all assumptions are faulty if there is not a research-validated curriculum being delivered with fidelity.

The question then becomes: What Tier One intervention are you using? That is where the focus turns back to the core curriculum and core instruction.

You have no business giving any student a Tier Two small group intervention until you have shown that your Tier one full-class instruction and curriculum has been:

1. Scientifically validated to work

2. Delivered with fidelity (and this has been documented in writing by an outside observer)

3. Shown to be ineffective for a particular student over a period of weeks, with over 8-10 different progress measurements.

Then, and only then, should anyone be talking about Tier Two small group interventions. Don't put the cart ahead of the horse.

One of the aspects that makes RTI effective is its emphasis on research-validated instructional techniques for ALL students.

 How are middle school and high school teachers supposed to find the time to deliver small group interventions? Teachers often have 150 students on their class lists!

When it comes to finding time to deliver Tier Two interventions at the secondary level, there are three models of delivery schools must choose from:

> **MODEL 1:**
> **Individual Teacher Delivers Intervention**
> **to His or Her Own Students**

This must be done during class time when the rest of the students are working on other activities or during another part of the day that both the student and the teacher have available. These "other times" might include before school, after school, lunch, study hall, or other free periods.

> **MODEL 2:**
> **Teachers Work Together to Deliver**
> **Subject-Area Interventions**

This model often takes the form of a "math lab" which is available all day or during key times (lunch periods, after school). Teachers and paraprofessionals rotate supervision of this area. When you are supervising the area, you deliver interventions to students regardless of whether or not you are their classroom teacher.

MODEL 3:
School-Wide Implementation

In this model, 20 to 30 minutes are set aside at the beginning or at the end of every day for students to receive interventions. Every teacher helps deliver these interventions.

Students who are not struggling either get a study hall, silent reading time, or gifted and talented activities.

 What is an example of an age-appropriate behavior education program at the elementary and secondary levels?

A good example of an elementary program is "Second Step to Success." This school-wide program has been shown to be effective.

At the secondary level, I recommend Vicki Phillips' curriculum "Personal Development." It is available in classroom format and in independent study format.

How many data points need to be considered before changing a Tier 2 intervention?

Most researchers agree that you should collect data at least twice a week for at least six weeks. Some people will suggest longer periods of time, but others will contend that more frequent data collecting (daily) can give you the information you need in fewer weeks. Twice a week for six weeks will give you twelve data points, which is a good number to target.

 Can I gather my progress monitoring data in a large group setting in math class?

Yes, math is more efficient than reading in this regard, and many teachers do it this way.

 Is Oral Reading Fluency the best measure of reading progress in grades 2 through 8? What about grades 9-12?

Oral Reading Fluency is certainly a good measure of reading progress, and it is one that is preferred by many teachers. The reasons for this are that Oral Reading Fluency is correlated with just about any indicator of good reading, and it takes just a few minutes to assess.

In grades 9 through 12, MAZE is commonly used for this purpose.

Parental Involvement and RTI

 How does parental involvement change when a school is implementing RTI?

Parents LOVE RTI when it is implemented correctly. Why?

Parents Want EARLY Communication

There is nothing worse than surprising a parent after nine weeks with bad news about their child. The student should not be surprised by this news, either. Best practice demands early communication (three to four weeks into the year) and communication from multiple sources (teacher, counselor, principal). Effective RTI implementation assures that problems are identified and addressed early and that parents are informed of this throughout the process. It should be apparent to the student and the parents that EVERYONE had noticed the trouble and is concerned about it.

Documentation Helps

Parents do not want generalizations—they want the details. This starts with a list of every missed assignment and every assessment score. Parents particularly like to see the median score of the class, which helps them put their child's score in perspective. More importantly, though, should be the documentation of the interventions you have used. This is where RTI really shines. You need to answer the "What have you tried?" question before parents even ask it. With RTI, you have not only documented the problem, you have also documented the interventions you have tried and the student's response to each intervention.

Parents Want Information in Writing

When I go to the doctor, I hear about half of what he says. I am nervous, I feel rushed, and I am distracted. Parents are the same way at conferences. Everything you say to parents — even little things like "homework tips" should also be given in written form so they can take it home and read it again later.

RTI is documented every step of the way:

- Universal Screening
- Full-Class Intervention
- Fidelity Check of Full-Class Intervention
- Progress Monitoring during Full-Class Intervention
- Small Group Intervention
- Fidelity Check of Small Group Intervention
- Progress Monitoring during Small Group Intervention

Parents Want to be Heard

Remember—your goal is to be successful with this student. If parents have changed their child's behavior so far, you can talk to the parents about this...but don't miss the real value of conferences. It is a great chance for you to learn more about the student and what motivates him or her. To learn this information, you must LISTEN as much as you talk. It also helps to ask good questions about what the student does outside of school and what has motivated them in the past. RTI creates multiple opportunities for you to listen.

 How do I get parents to "buy-in" to the RTI process?

RTI is sweeping across the nation because it solves problems. RTI keeps trying different solutions until we find one that works. How do you convey this to parents? I suggest using a simple strategy called: Quick-Hitters.

This strategy is so successful I try to use it at least a dozen times in each grading period.

Basically, the strategy is to share with parents a problem that you have already identified, intervened, and solved. It doesn't have to be a big problem, but it needs to be successfully solved by the time you talk to parents.

The script sounds like this:

"Hi, Mr. and Mrs. _____. A few weeks ago, I noticed that your son, _____, was struggling with _____. I tried _____. That seems to have worked and now your son is doing a great job in that area."

Here is an example with the blanks filled in:

"A few weeks ago, I noticed that Brandon was struggling with remembering to bring his pencil to class. I told him to try leaving a pencil tucked in his folder. That seems to be working—he is bringing a pencil to all of his classes now!"

It seems so simple. Why does it work?

- First, it builds parents' confidence in your ability to identify and solve problems.

- Second, it is a great way to show how well you know their child.

- Third, when you do suggest a solution to a new larger problem, they will be more likely to trust your suggested solution. Why not? After all, you have been successful in the past!

Sometimes, I will go as far as solving very small problems - messy folders, dull pencils, shoes untied - with one of my great solutions just so I have an anecdote to share with parents. I always make a note when I do this so that I remember to share the story with parents at conference time.

Try this strategy—it works!

Eligibility

 What is the difference between using RTI for eligibility and using RTI for helping students succeed?

Many people are confused about this issue. There are two different ways that a school or district can implement RTI:

- One way is to simply use RTI to help struggling students succeed.

- The second way is to do that, but ALSO use RTI to determine eligibility for special education services.

Oftentimes when I am speaking at a conference about Response to Intervention, I will sense negativity from teachers about RTI in general. One of the reasons for this negative attitude is that schools are implementing all of the bad parts of RTI (paperwork, increased responsibilities, etc.) without all of the benefits.

One of the biggest benefits of using Response to Intervention in any school is using it for Special Education Eligibility. When used correctly, it is a faster, easier, and better way to identify students with learning disabilities and to get them the services they need and deserve.

Many schools are making the teachers jump through the hoops of RTI without giving them the benefits at the back end. Although a Response to Intervention approach will help all students by giving them targeted quality interventions, to stop there is to miss the finish line by a few steps. Why not go all the way and reward teachers and students by giving them a process to determine eligibility, as well?

Here are some common issues surrounding using RTI for eligibility purposes:

Insofar as eligibility goes, kids qualify for special education services when a scientifically validated Tier 2 small group intervention has been implemented with fidelity and the student does not make measurable progress after having received the intervention. (The student did not "respond" to the intervention—hence the name RTI!) All of these steps should be documented: The initial identification screening, the full-class Tier 1 intervention, the progress monitoring, the small group Tier 2 intervention, the progress monitoring, and the observation of the intervention being implemented (fidelity check).

After that happens, the student certainly qualifies. If you are going to use this system, you do NOT need to run a full battery of discrepancy tests as was done in the past. To do so would be to have duplicate systems and waste valuable resources.

The number of interventions that you try is not as important as whether or not they are targeted correctly. Certainly, the classroom teacher should have tried some things with her class (Tier 1 full-class interventions.) Then, the teacher should try a targeted Tier 2 intervention and follow the steps above. You are welcome to try another intervention after that one, but it is not required.

By "Targeted" intervention, I mean that it is aligned with the problem. If the student is struggling with reading fluency, make sure your intervention targets that, not just beginning letter sounds.

If your Tier 2 intervention is targeted correctly, delivered correctly, and progress is monitored correctly, the student has "not responded to a scientifically validated intervention" and that information should be used to determine eligibility.

IDEA 2004 specifies that, for the purpose of determining learning disability eligibility, a school district may implement a procedure that involves documentation "based on the child's response to scientific, research-based intervention."

There are two other things I should mention:

First, your state should have RTI eligibility criteria, and you should check those. Many states do not have them yet, but they are required to develop them. Criteria vary greatly from state to state in regard to timing, documentation, etc. Some states have done a great job making this a usable process. Other states have hampered teachers' efforts by making the process completely unusable.

Second, IDEA 2004 also states that:

> To ensure that underachievement in a child suspected of having a specific learning disability is not due to

lack of appropriate instruction in reading or math, the group must consider, as part of the evaluation...(1) Data that demonstrate that prior to, or as a part of, the referral process, the child was provided appropriate instruction in regular education settings, delivered by qualified personnel; and (2) Data-based documentation of repeated assessments of achievement at reasonable intervals, reflecting formal assessment of student progress during instruction, which was provided to the child's parents.

Of course, you always want to be evaluating the quality of instruction and you always want to communicate progress with parents...so keep it up!

 ## Why is using RTI for eligibility purposes so important?

The original idea behind RTI was that it would be used instead of a discrepancy model to identify students for special education services. When it is, it opens up free time for school psychologists and certain special education staff because they are no longer performing a long battery of tests to see if students were eligible. The original concept was that these people would use their newly obtained free time to help teachers with progress monitoring and recording.

NOTE to the people who invented RTI: This free time has apparently disappeared.

Many schools are implementing RTI, but maintaining a discrepancy model...Bad Idea, but they are doing it anyway. Even if they have given up the discrepancy model, the free time that the school psychologist and the special education staff were supposed to have has disappeared. To be implemented correctly, RTI requires that you reallocate the way that you use certain staff members. To implement RTI without doing this is a recipe for a difficult transition to RTI.

 Isn't RTI really just "tracking" or "ability-grouping"?

If students were being removed from their regular instruction to be placed in remedial instruction, I would worry about tracking or ability grouping...but that is not really part of RTI as most schools implement it.

Tier One full-class interventions are delivered to the full class— so there is no risk of tracking there. You are simply using a research-validated curriculum or teaching method to your heterogeneous group of students, and closely monitoring the progress of a select group of students in the class.

Tier Two small group interventions are often done in addition to the full-class instruction. The downside of tracking is that students are never exposed to higher-level material and have little chance to be surrounded by successful, positive role models. Neither of these two negatives occurs when the Tier Two small group intervention is implemented in addition to full-class instruction.

The other way to implement Tier Two small group interventions is to do them instead of the regular instruction. There would be a risk of tracking here if the goal of the intervention was not to move the student back to the larger full class. Tracking happens when you pull out a group of low-achieving or low-ability students and keep them in a group indefinitely. That will never happen with RTI. The students will either respond to the intervention (in which case, they learn, improve, and eventually are back at peer-level) or they will not respond to the intervention (in which case, you move on to a more intensive Tier Three intervention).

There is no risk of a student being sentenced to a full year of being "stuck" in a low-ability, low-achieving, slow-moving class full of poor role models. The student will either be learning or the intensity of the intervention will be increased.

This is just another reason why the RTI model is so much better than the traditional "discrepancy model" when it comes to addressing student needs. In the old model, a student labeled "behind" could languish for years in "tracked" remedial classes. The damage of this tracking is well documented. In a properly implemented RTI model, that can never happen. A student will either "respond" by learning and improving, or the intervention is changed.

In Tier Three, we are delivering specialized services. It has been decided that for this group of students, the benefits of receiving these much-needed services outweigh the grouping that occurs, as long as the services are delivered in the least restrictive environment possible.

In my mind, students have a much better chance of being successful if you are watching how they respond to interventions, and changing your intervention if you find that one is not working!

SECTION THREE

RTI IN ACTION:

REAL EXAMPLES FROM REAL CLASSROOMS

25 Teachers Share Their...

Tier One Full-Class Intervention Examples

I use *Open Court Reading* resources with full class.

Accelerated Reader is the only scientifically valid intervention used with my entire class.

We use *Houghton Mifflin Reading* as our Tier 1 intervention.

Our entire school uses *Accelerated Reader* for reading. We also use Personal Development for character education.

I use *Everyday Math.*

For Reading instruction, we use *Imagine it,* by Open Court, published by Science Research Associates.

Our school uses *Houghton Mifflin Math Expressions.*
SRA Real Math.

Fastt Math is the best Tier 1 or Tier 2 Math intervention I have ever used.

Read Naturally.

Reading Recovery.

Accelerated Reader is the easiest way to individualize reading for your full class.

For behavior, I use Vicki Phillip's *Personal Development* with my full class.

Ignite! Learning provides technology-based math, science, and social studies curriculum. Each course offers 3 years of middle school curriculum tied to state standards.

Math Trailblazers is a research-based program that includes math, science, and reading skills. Students using Math Trailblazers are actively engaged in real-world situations to practice problem-solving strategies. This program includes a balance of group work, individual work, and whole-class instruction.

Our campus uses *Accelerated Reader/Reading Renaissance* and *SuccessMaker.*

I use *Lessons in Character.*

Best Practices Behavior Interventions- This deals with how to handle ED students, as well as other defiant students.

I use Read Naturally.

We use *literary circles,* and the kids love it!

Boys Town Well Managed Classroom and *PBS (Positive Behavior Support)* are used.

For math class, we use *Bridges in Mathematics.*

We use the *AR system* (Accelerated Reader).

Our school uses *reachout.com* to teach about common thinking errors.

We use *successmaker* at our school.

25 Teachers Share Their...

Tier Two Small Group Intervention Examples

If a student identified with the universal screening does not make progress after 6 weeks of my Tier One full-class intervention, I use a Tier Two intervention. I have 4 students who are currently using *Read Naturally* as a Tier Two intervention in reading.

For students who do not progress with large group intervention, I offer *Small group instruction* and practice with addition and subtraction in the back of the room with me.

I use *Fasttmath* with my students who do not respond to the Tier One intervention.

We use *Reading Recovery* in reading and *Fasttmath* in math.

If my progress monitoring shows that students are not progressing during my full-class instruction, I put them in *Small group instruction* (done by a parent volunteer) using manipulatives to teach fact families in math.

Our school uses all three reading programs developed by Lindamood Bell Learning Processes: *Seeing Stars, LiPS and Visualizing and Verbalizing.*

> I am using *Peer Assisted Tutoring* regularly as a Tier 2 intervention. I have access to native-speakers; since this approach is cost-free, it helps me and helps the students needing additional interventions.

When the full-class instruction fails to produce progress in reading, we use *Ignite!learning* with the smaller subset of students.

We use *Successmaker* for supplemental instruction in English, language arts, math, science, and social studies.

Read Naturally – it is the best and easiest small group reading program to use.

I use *Florida Center for Reading Research* activities with small groups of students who are not making adequate progress with my full-class instruction.

Signs for Sounds is a phonics-through-spelling program that has been very successful for my students who did not respond to the Tier One intervention.

I identify students early in the year using a universal screening method. I monitor the progress of these students throughout the first six weeks of math instruction. Students who fail to make progress (as viewed on their individual graph) will receive Tier Two services using *Math Trailblazers*.

When students are not making adequate progress or measurable progress, I often work in *small groups* with my students when studying the writing process (6 traits of writing).

If my progress monitoring graph does not show a line going up and to the right, I work with *small groups of students to break down steps into smaller steps*.

> For behavior, I use the individualized version of *Personal Development*. I can pick or choose lessons based on what the student is struggling with. You do not have to do the lessons in any order, which I love.

Students who don't move forward with my full-class instruction get additional Tier Two interventions using Saxon Middle School Math and *SuccessMaker*.

We use *Read Naturally* after a student has failed to "raise the line" on their graph for more than four weeks.

We use Nanci Bell's *Visualizing and Verbalizing For Language Comprehension and Thinking® Program* as a Tier 2 small group intervention in Language Arts.

The *Fast ForWord* program is a reading intervention designed for all grades K-12. We use it as our primary Tier Two English and Language Arts intervention at the high school level. Middle Schools and Elementary Schools in our district use it, as well.

I have done some *small group fluency* instruction and practice with my students based on our textbook.

Nanci Bell's *Seeing Stars: Symbol Imagery for Phonemic Awareness, Sight Words and Spelling Program* (Seeing Stars) is a Tier Two intervention designed to instruct and improve students' phonemic awareness, sight word knowledge, and spelling through the development of symbol imagery.

When students struggle to learn, we use *Buckle Down* practice books in small groups.

Our school uses *Orton Gillingham multi-sensory methods* in small groups.

We use *Skilltutor* with our small groups of students who struggle with any particular skill. It is so easy to individualize the instruction to the deficiency. We are a middle school, but I know that our high school and elementary schools use it, as well.

50 Teachers Share Their…

Progress Monitoring Examples

I test students with reading passages first thing in the morning. All of our students are held in the main hallway from the time they are dropped off until 7:30 a.m. Two of my students know that on Monday they can come directly to my room when they get dropped off (usually around 7:15 or 7:20) to be tested. Two different students do this each day of the week (Monday through Thursday), so I can test all eight of the students who I identified with my universal screening. Fridays are left over for students who were absent or who arrived late on their day.

I do a 5-minute timing tool for lower addition and subtraction facts to 10. It is easy to graph and analyze their progress.

We use *Renaissance Learning* at our school, so the STAR test and the Accelerated Reader program does this for me.

I'm giving two timed tests each week to determine if my students are mastering their basic addition and subtraction facts. The kids are given 2 minutes to try to complete 40 basic facts. I record scores in a grade book and graph the progress of the group of students I am "watching."

I teach middle school and use oral reading passages. I graph the score of certain students twice each week. It quickly becomes obvious who is progressing and who is not.

I give a weekly spelling test for all in my high reading group. If the children pass the words, they will not be given them again the next week. If they miss some words, I will repeat the words. I then review words at regular intervals. I record these grades in the grade book and graph the progress of certain students.

Our middle school uses *Renaissance Learning's* STAR reading assessments.

I record comprehension grades each week and graph the grades of a select group of students.

In Reading, I use *DIBELS/IRI*.

I check my students' progress with reading vocabulary word lists each day right before lunch. I have declared the last 10 minutes before lunch to be study hall or silent reading time. This way, I can check three or four students each day. Right now, I am only monitoring the progress of 6 students, so they each get a mark on their graph at least twice a week, sometimes three times. It only takes two minutes per student. I was afraid this would not work, but when I tried it, I found it works great. The "study hall" right before lunch is easy to manage, because if you are off task, you go to lunch late. Trust me – no one is off task!

In Math, I use 1-Minute Timings three times each week. I graph the results…it is almost easier than recording them in my gradebook. I use Pat Quinn's one-page graph for each student I am monitoring.

I also do Progress Monitoring Dibels in my class because their fluency levels are pretty low.

Our first and second grade students are monitored with *Fox and the Box Reading Assessment.*

In math, I do three minute timings for basic multiplication and division facts. I do multiplication one week and then division the next week.

I check my students' oral reading fluency each week and graph the results of certain students using Pat Quinn's clipboard idea.

Twice each week, I use number writing to 100 and addition facts to 10. I graph the results for students identified with our Universal Screening.

I have a parent volunteer fill out observational behavior report cards on three different students twice each week. They observe each student for 20 minutes, so on Tuesday I use my parent volunteer for one hour to do this. Same thing on Thursday. It is a great way to utilize a parent volunteer!

I teach high school and we use *STAR Math* with our at-risk students. Our middle school uses the same system so it is a smooth transition from grade 5 to 12.

In Math, I use 2-minute fact assessments on Mondays, Wednesdays and Fridays.

I use our county benchmarks for facts and application *FASTT Math STAR* Math 100 fact check in 6 min. for addition and subtraction.

In Reading, I use *DIBELS*.

I teach ninth grade and use *STAR* reading assessments with all of our students. It actually identifies who is ready for the next Tier. We have used them all and this is the one that works best with RTI.

We are using *Skillstutor* for our Tier Two interventions, so it really keeps track of student progress for us.

In Reading, I use *Yellow Box*.

Our school uses *Read Naturally* with students who struggle.

I use behavior report cards.

We use *STAR Reading* from Accelerated Reader.

I mostly use *Houghton Mifflin Assessments Selection Tests.*

I use a 5-minute writing probe and Daily Oral Language.

In Language Arts, I will use *Performance Tasks Writing Rubrics* with all students, then carefully monitor the students identified as "at-risk" to see if they need further intervention.

My Spanish students have a list of 20 words to read aloud. I graph the results weekly.

Our school uses *Aimsweb.*

In math, I use one minute basic fact tests.

I use *DIBELS* progress monitoring.

I use vocabulary word lists and graph the results using the clipboard graphing method described in Pat Quinn's video course.

Math - flash card drills and written drills - both 1 minute.

Dibels Daily 5.

91

I hold individual conferences for reading and writing. My 3rd grade students read silently or do a different independent activity while I do this.

I use *Successmaker* to monitor progress.

I use the built in monitoring sheets for documentation in the reading fluency program in place in class.

I use oral reading samples and graph the results.

I teach high school and use a behavior check list. I graph the results at the end of each week. Takes about 5 minutes.

I can do quick oral (or written) vocab quizzes with the student.

I use *Dibels*.

We use the *STAR* test for Math.

I use *Aimsweb*. It does much of the work for me!

Math - one minute basic facts in four operation areas.

In reading, I use *Dibels* - reading rate and accuracy 4-sight.

In Reading, I use *Fox in the Box*. It is the best assessment I have found K-2.

Our school uses *Edusoft*.

25 Teachers Share Their...

RTI Time Management Tips and Examples

In the beginning, it seemed like I could never find the time to do the interventions and progress monitoring that I needed to. After a couple semesters, you get into a pattern where it just "fits" into your day – then you wonder what all the worrying was about! My best technique is to pull kids to the back of the room (not the front) as soon as I give an assignment and everyone begins working. Then, I can check the progress of that one student, record it on his or her graph, and send them back to their desk before students start to get squirrelly. I do this 4-5 times each day. It works for me!

I do it individually with each student in a 1-1 session. It can be done in the classroom or as a pullout while the rest of my class is doing other things.

Edusoft is a part of grading the tests so does not take extra time. As the RTI person in the middle school, I pull students out of class three times a week to monitor progress.

I review classroom procedures with the students and have them work on independent class work while I go around the room and monitor the progress of my struggling students.

> I use a clipboard graphing system as Pat Quinn recommends in his online class, so it only takes a couple minutes per day, but I add a place for notes on the back of each sheet. These notes become my written documentation when we use RTI for eligibility.

I divide students into 2 groups during class time to measure progress. One group is working independently, while the other group works with me.

I teach middle school, and I have five students in my first class who are on behavior report cards. It is their responsibility to bring the card up to me at the end of each day to get it signed. Their parents sign it each night. At the end of the week, I graph the results.

The *Computer for Successmaker* does it for me, the student works on it while the rest of the class is reading.

Daily Oral Language is done at the beginning of writing class every day and it is reviewed every week, on Fridays.

Dibels is done monthly; quick writes and math fluency are done every other week. *Daily 5* is done 2 times a week.

I have a paraprofessional help me with *Dibels*.

My math progress monitoring I do with the full class – it is just easier that way and I benefit from the extra data.

I use a Title 1 paraprofessional to help with the reading interventions and progress monitoring.

Some of the "quick writes" that I do are used with the full class. They only take 3 minutes.

I do it while students are involved in partner or group activities. I usually have a student read a list while we are working on speaking/ listening exercises.

Have the class work on a project of some sort while I pull kids to the back table to test.

I have a parent give these timings in math and graph the results. They appreciate the chance to work with specific students repeatedly.

During *IRI* timings and *Dibels*, we are fortunate to have specialists and instructional assistants in our rooms so students are on tasks while others are being tested. I do not have a paraprofessional available during Math timings – I give those while others are working independently or in small groups.

I have several parent volunteers who could also give the math tests I need to administer.

I do the timings, I write scores and progress on graph paper, but do not "graph" it. I share daily progress, actually from day before, with the students.

I administer the timings and volunteers correct the timings.

For Progress Monitoring, I test the students when the rest of the class is silent reading. That way I can work with one student at a time without having to find busy work for the rest of the class.

I look throughout the day for "strategic opportunities" to test students. I can usually find 3 or 4 times each day where everyone is working quietly on something for a few minutes so I can do this.

I do all their Math Measures myself. Math 2 minute fact assessments—every 2 weeks county benchmarks for facts and application.

Appendix One

Response to Intervention for Middle Schools and High Schools

Many people believe that Response to Intervention is an elementary program and not appropriate for implementation at the middle school or high school level. This is simply not the case. Many schools around the county are having great success implementing RTI at the secondary level, BUT KNOW THIS:

RTI looks different that the secondary level than it does at the elementary school level.

Many districts follow a very predictable pattern of failure. They begin by implementing RTI at the elementary level in reading. They see some success, so they expand to math and possible behavioral issues. After this success, they decide to expand RTI to the secondary level. Sometimes this decision is not really a choice; your state tells you that you must implement RTI in all grades K-12.

The mistake districts make is to follow the same model of RTI at the secondary level that worked for them at the elementary level. This is a recipe for a failed implementation of RTI. Response to Intervention must look different in your middle school and high school than it does at your elementary schools. If you do not begin with this in mind, you will have a disaster on your hands.

How many times have middle school and high school teachers attended professional development presentations that were geared toward elementary school teachers? Every veteran secondary school teacher has horror stories of sitting through full presentations designed by and designed for elementary school teachers. You soon begin to recognize this problem and learn to quickly shut off the speaker and think about other things.

The same is true with RTI. If you approach your teachers with a program that looks like it is designed for elementary school students, elementary school teachers, and an elementary school schedule—your teachers will shut you off like a faucet.

Instead, we are looking for RTI to be implemented in a way that fits the secondary schedule, a secondary teacher's student load, and the limits of a secondary school system.

Let's go through the steps of RTI paying special emphasis to how each step looks at the secondary level.

Step One: Universal Screening

The universal screening is the first place that RTI starts to look different on the secondary level than it does on the elementary level. At the elementary level, we may administer a reading test to all students three or four times during a school year to identify students who are having a particular difficulty. At the middle school or high school level, the students come to us with a wealth of data on who is having difficulty. Most secondary schools who are successfully implementing RTI do not administer a separate universal screening. Instead, they utilize data that already exists to identify which students to monitor more closely during the next phase.

Step Two: Tier One Full-Class Instruction

At the secondary level, Tier One looks like a teacher teaching a full class of students. I would assume most of your teachers are doing that already – so I think you have this one covered!

But do not move on too quickly…a couple of things we should check:

First, is the curriculum that the teacher is using a research-validated curriculum? Remember, the bar has been raised here from "research-based" to "research proven." Double-check to make sure that the curriculum being used meets this criteria. This is a one-time check that can be done at the school or district level.

Second, is the teacher making accommodations for student differences? You can call this "differentiated instruction" if you want, but I prefer to refer to it as simply "good teaching." Students in middle school and high school have a broad range of differences, including background information, rate of learning, and learning style. The classroom teacher should be accommodating of as many of these as possible.

Remember: Response to Intervention will not be successful in any school if the Tier One Full-Class Instruction is not being successful with at least 75% of the students. That's right, if more than 1 in 4 students is unsuccessful in class, you should not implement RTI at your middle school or high school. Instead, you should focus on improving classroom instruction to get to that level.

There is not a school that I know that has the resources, room, or people necessary to implement RTI if more than one in four students is failing during full-class instruction. You simply cannot deliver small group or one-on-one interventions to that many students.

If the regular classroom teacher is having success using a research-validated curriculum and accommodating individual needs in the classroom, you have Tier One covered.

Step Three: Fidelity Check During Tier One Full-Class Instruction

Most teachers that I know are observed during the school year by an administrator. This is a check to see if the curriculum is being taught correctly and, if documented, can be used as the Tier One Fidelity Check.

If you are not being observed by an administrator, ask a colleague or specialist from your school to observe your teaching and document the observation. Secondary schools are actually set up better for peer observation in many cases than elementary schools because colleagues who teach the same subject may have different free periods available for observation.

Step Four: Progress Monitoring During Tier One

Certain students were identified using a universal screening or existing data. These students should have their progress monitored during the full-class instruction. This will look differently based on what initial deficiency was identified. Here are some examples:

A ninth-grade math teacher recognizes that two students lack the prerequisite skills in the area of fractions. Twice each week she gives those two students a short fraction assessment to see if those skills are improving. This is done in class by the classroom teacher while other students are working on their assignments. This data is recorded and graphed over time.

A seventh-grade Language Arts teacher sees before the school year even begins that he has four students who are reading well below grade level. He administers a short reading comprehension check once each week to these four students. Usually, he finds a time during class to do this; sometimes he needs to pull them out of lunch for the last 10 minutes to do this. This data is recorded and graphed over time.

A high school U.S. History teacher has three students who lack organizational skills and self-control in class. The teacher records every day whether these three students are on time, have proper supplies, have completed assignments, remain in their seats, and take notes. This data is recorded and graphed over time.

All of these examples have something in common: regular monitoring to see if the chosen intervention is effective. Too many times, we select a remedial intervention for a student and leave them in it for a semester or a year, regardless of its effectiveness. That is not RTI. RTI continually asks the question: Is this intervention working?

There are specific steps that teachers are taking at the secondary school level to help students and implement RTI. Let's look separately at what schools are doing in Reading, Math, and General Study and Organizational Skills.

Reading:

As No Child Left Behind starts to ratchet up the pressure, middle schools and high schools around the country are doing everything they can to help readers achieve grade level proficiency.

Because the student's traditional courses are already packed with content, teachers are hesitant (or unable because of the wide span of abilities) to provide targeted reading instruction because it would come at the expense of other content that must be covered.

For this reason, schools are taking students who are reading well below grade level (or not reading at all) and providing them additional reading instruction during another part of their day. Depending on your schedule, this additional instruction may happen before school, during study hall, during lunch, after school, or in the evening.

This instruction is most effective if it is individualized and self-paced. Schools use reading specialists, teachers, paraprofessionals and computer-aided instruction to provide this extra support.

Oftentimes, students must give up taking an elective class (or delay taking a specific class) to make room for this extra instruction. Schools should not feel bad forcing a student to do this because they know the additional reading instruction will help the student in every aspect of their academics.

Math:

Traditionally, math classes are a bit more ability-grouped at the high school level, with students taking algebra, geometry, or pre-algebra.

At the high school level when students are not yet ready for algebra, schools are increasingly finding it ineffective to continue teaching a traditional pre-algebra class. There are many reasons why this is ineffective, including the fact that this mode of instruction has been shown to be less effective for this particular group of students.

Instead, what many schools are doing is an individualized self-paced curriculum that focuses specifically on the deficiencies that a student has that is causing them to be unable to succeed in algebra.

If you have 25 ninth grade students who lack the prerequisite skills to take algebra, my guess is that each of them is lacking a different set of skills. Some may be missing fractions. Some may be missing negatives. Some may be missing exponents. Some may be missing all of the above.

Because they are all missing different skills, why would we put them all through the same remediation?

The student who lacks only fraction skills should focus on fractions. The student who lacks only positive/negative skills should focus on negatives. You get the idea.

So instead of walking classrooms full of students lock-step through a pre-algebra course, schools have taken the same group of students and individualized the instruction.

Using a pre-test to measure what skills they lack, an individual course of study is designed to help them be ready for algebra. Most schools find by using this method you can prepare a student to be ready for algebra in one semester rather than one year. (Of course, your schedule may not allow students to begin algebra in January, but that is another matter.)

Some schools deliver the individualized instruction using computer-aided instruction with great programs such as Skillstutor. Visit www.skillstutor.com for more information.

Other schools have "modularized" their pre-algebra curriculum into packets or "modules" so that students can focus on just the areas they need the most help, with the teacher delivering one-on-one or small-group help when needed.

In the end, you will see these results:

- ✓ Students will be prepared for algebra faster because they won't be sitting through instruction on topics they already understand.

- ✓ Behavior problems go down, because students are not bored in a self-paced curriculum.

✓ Effort and attendance go up because the amount of time the student spends in the class is directly related to how hard they work and the competency level they show.

✓ Success in algebra goes up because students need to show competency in all areas before taking the class. (In the old method, getting great grades in some chapters of pre-algebra could mask incompetence in other areas.)

✓ Graduation rates and college enrollment rates go up when you have a program that helps students pass algebra.

Not a bad target to shoot for if you ask me!

General Study and Organizational Skills:

In a more general sense, there are also many schools implementing Tier 1 and Tier 2 interventions focusing on cross-curricular skills, such as organization and motivation.

Schools all over the country are flocking to Vicki Phillip's "Personal Development" curriculum for its wealth of student activities research proven to increase student self-esteem, organizational skills, goal-setting and learning. Check it out at www.personaldevelopment.org.

Even with tightly packed schedules, teachers are finding the time to implement specific classroom wide and small-group interventions because they know that time spent on these foundational skills will pay off for years to come.

Don't let anyone fool you into thinking that helping students with essential organizational, note-taking, memorization, and time management skills is outside your curriculum. It is not. It is this very set of skills that your curriculum was originally developed to enhance and develop.

Middle School and High School Interventions

What do RTI interventions actually look like at the high school level?

Remember this simple rule:

Interventions always include additional instruction.

And so, regardless of how the student is struggling, we are going to add additional instruction to the student (targeted at the specific root cause that's causing them to be unsuccessful).

For instance, if the student is struggling in Social Studies class because they aren't reading, then we want a reading intervention (additional reading instruction). It can certainly be reading instruction within the content area of Social Studies, but it will always be reading instruction/additional instructional minutes.

If the student is struggling in Science class because they lack a math background that is sufficient to succeed in the class that they're in, then we want to target that with additional math instruction.

And if the student lacks organizational skills or the ability to control their behavior in class, we want to target additional instruction and behavioral interventions after that.

So when does all this instruction take place?

The truth is: if you're not willing to adjust your schedule – the schedule of your school – to create time for these interventions, RTI implementation will not be successful at your school.

Let me give you some examples of specific times that people implement instructional interventions for students who are struggling in class.

The first is the simplest: the classroom teacher finds time in class to deliver additional instruction.

When would this happen? Well, in certain classes, there are times when the class works—when they do independent practice. During this time, some teachers have it all together and can actually deliver additional instruction to certain students during this work time. That's the simplest, it's the easiest, and it should be the first step in any RTI plan—that additional instruction is delivered during class by the classroom teacher.

Next step: Many students have a study hall, and this study hall is often free time with no instruction delivered. The next step would be to change that from a non-instructional time to instructional time – that the student could get help in a specific area (targeted to their specific deficiency) during this time.

Schools often implement this in two stages.

The first stage is to switch the student from just a supervised study hall to a monitored study hall. They recognize that certain students lack the organizational skills and, the skills of getting started on assignments, completing assignments, and organizing which assignments should get done first.

A monitored study hall is a simple way to put students in a slightly smaller group (instead of groups of 30, 40, or 50, maybe groups of 20) with an adult who is going to do more than sit there and correct papers while they study. This person is actually going to monitor what they are working on and ask each student as they come in, "What are you going to be working on today? What assignments do you have due later today or due tomorrow that you would like to work on?"

This changes the idea of study hall from a supervised time to a monitored time.

The second stage would be to change this time into an instructional time—to actually pair up students who are struggling in math with a math teacher in their study hall, to pair up students who are struggling in reading with a language arts teacher in their study hall, and to pair up students who are struggling to control their behavior (or with organizational or personal skills) with an instructor who's qualified to deliver organizational skills or behavior modification programs to the students during this time.

Now we have three different types of "study hall."

The first is for students who aren't struggling: they're in a study hall that is supervised (certainly by an adult), but there's no instruction delivered.

The second is a monitored study hall, where the work is monitored ("What are you working on today? Are you getting started? Are you working it to completion?").

The third is targeted by subject area and the specific deficiency to put in an instructor who is ready to teach that subject – to help students with math, help students with reading, or help students with their behavior – during that study hall time.

This is a movement of adult personnel within the student schedule (which really doesn't change that much in this model), and we are utilizing our adult personnel differently during this model.

The next question usually is, "What do you do if you don't have study hall built into your schedule or if your students don't have a study hall?" There are additional times during the school day that you can make available for additional instruction for students. These times might include: half of their lunch period (and, of course, if you're in a district or a state that doesn't allow you to remove lunch from students, you can make instruction available to students during lunch without forcing them into it), times before school and after school (many schools use 30 minutes before school or 30 minutes after school as an additional intervention instructional time), in the evening (and many schools allow parents to come in, as well, to have access to the school library, to the school computers, and to additional English language instruction, if you have parents who don't speak English.), and on Saturdays. These are all opportunities that different schools are utilizing to deliver additional instruction.

Remember this when implementing RTI: At some point, you will need to deliver additional instruction to struggling students. Don't fight this, embrace it...and be creative to find a way to deliver!

Conclusion

Is implementing RTI at the middle school or high school level a good idea? The answer is "no" if you are just going to copy an elementary school model. The answer is a definitive "yes" if you are going to work within your high school system to create an environment where struggling students get the help that they need.

Appendix Two

Getting RTI Started Quickly at Your School

The question is a simple one:

What is the fastest way to get RTI started at my school?

The answer, unfortunately, is not that simple.

To successfully implement Response to Intervention at any school, we need to understand three rules—three imperatives that will always be present.

Rule #1:
RTI looks different in different schools.

The first is: **RTI looks different in different schools.** Although this statement seems obvious, it clearly is not, because so many schools that I go into that are trying to implement Response to Intervention are copying a neighboring school's model and trying to shoehorn it into their school. But their school has different students, different subjects, different schedules, different teachers, and a different culture.

So, don't go out and make a carbon copy of another school's model, and certainly don't look at an elementary school model if you are working in a middle school or high school. Visit other schools and read about other schools at your level. Then pick and choose the ideas that fit the best in your school.

Rule #2:
An intervention involves instruction.

The second rule that we want to follow is this: **An intervention involves instruction.** This is an extremely important rule to follow, because I go in a lot of schools where there are many of what they call "interventions" in place, but the interventions are:

"We put you on a list."

"We call your parents."

"We put you in a room."

"We take away half of your lunch."

"We do all these things, but it never involves instruction."

By its very definition, an intervention involves additional instruction, and if you're not ready to add additional instructional minutes in certain subjects to certain students' days, then you're not ready for Response to Intervention at your school.

Interventions involve instruction. All the other things that we do—all the phone calls, all of the warning lists, all of the watch lists, all the meetings—all the things we do to help catch kids

112

that are falling through the cracks are great, but they are not interventions unless they involve additional minutes of instruction, unless they involve more *teaching*.

Rule #3:
Root Causes Matter

The third rule that we're going to follow as we implement Response to Intervention is: **Root causes matter.**

It really does matter what a root cause of a student's problem is. We are not going to be successful with a student in class, no matter what instructional interventions we have in place, if the student has an existing drug and alcohol problem. We are not going to be successful with a student, regardless of the academic interventions that we put in place, if the student can't control his own behavior, can't concentrate, or has power struggle issues.

There are a host of root causes that we must understand and identify with students that we work with, and, until we do this, all the interventions in the world aren't going to make a difference, but when we do this, we can target the correct intervention to the correct student.

Again and again and again, we're going to ask the teachers, the counselors, the assistant principals—everybody who works with our students who are not being successful—to not just look at and identify the problem, but we also want them to identify the root cause, and that is what we are going to go after with our interventions.

And so, if you follow these three rules; if you recognize that RTI will look different at different schools, if you understand that interventions will always include additional instructional minutes, and if you keep looking for root causes, then we're on our way to successfully implementing RTI at the high school level.

Getting Started Quickly

So, what is the best way to "jumpstart" RTI at your school once you understand these three rules?

Follow these simple steps:

Get teachers the data they need

Improve full-class instruction

Teach teachers to collect and use data

Create a system for small-group interventions

If you can do those four steps, you are 90% of the way to implementing RTI. Everything else is just tweaking and improving. Let's go over each step in more detail.

Step One:
Get Teachers the Data They Need

No one could argue that we do not gather enough data on our students. Most schools are drowning in test scores and other data. The problem is that teachers often don't have access to the data they need.

For instance, on the first day of school a typical teacher will have 25 students sitting in front of them in class. Prior to that day, have they been given easy-to-use access to the students' deficiencies, both individually and as a group of 25 students? Often, the answer is no.

Prior to the first day of school, teachers should have data to identify which students might struggle and which students should be monitored more closely. Once this data is given to teachers, they should be expected to use it to drive instruction.

Step Two:
Improve Full-Class Instruction

The easiest and fastest way to increase learning in a school is to increase full-class instruction. Most experts in RTI will agree that if classroom instruction is not being successful with 75% of students, then you are not ready to implement RTI.

Focus your full-class instruction improvement efforts on three areas:

Research-validated curriculum. Make sure the core curriculum you are using in each subject area is research-proven to work. Use websites such as www.w-w-c.org to check for validation.

Differentiation. On any given day, if every student in the classroom is doing the exact same activity, the teacher is not maximizing learning in the classroom. Both the teacher and the students need to become comfortable with different students doing different activities and having different assignments on a given day.

Instructional Methods. When a teacher uses the same method to instruct every single day, learning will not be maximized. Whether it is lecture, discussion, read the textbook, watch my PowerPoint, or showing a movie, teachers cannot use the same method every day. Work with teachers to expand their menu of options for instruction for kids so that ALL students can benefit.

Step Three:
Teach Teachers to Collect and Use Data

Here is where the rubber meets the road with RTI. Teachers need to be able to collect progress-monitoring data on student learning.

The key to RTI is teachers deciding whether or not the interventions they are using are effective or not. Too many times, we implement an intervention, and we keep using it for six months or a year, never paying any attention to whether it is working or not.

Teachers need to be taught and trained in this skill. They did not learn it in college. In most cases, it has not been required of them in the past.

More specifically, the steps they should learn include:

- ✓ Identifying the skill they want to measure
- ✓ Choosing a tool to measure the skill
- ✓ Recording the results from the measurement
- ✓ Making a decision on effectiveness.

You will need to dedicate a great deal of professional development time to this specific area, but it is worth it. RTI will not be successfully implemented in your school until teachers can do this.

One book that has been a valuable resource in helping teachers learn this skill is *The ABC's of CBM* by Michelle Hosp and friends. It sits on my desk and is a great resource.

Step Four:
Create a System for Small-Group Interventions

If you want RTI to happen at your school, you should not expect teachers to find and acquire their own small-group interventions. To really jumpstart RTI and get the ball rolling, the school or district should select and provide the small group interventions in reading, writing, math, and behavior skills.

These small group interventions will often be purchased programs. Depending on how and when they are implemented, it may also require additional personnel to be provided to do the implementation.

You will also need to provide time in the schedule for small group interventions.

When teachers are locked into a rigid schedule with no time to offer students extra instruction, they feel helpless and powerless. In this situation, the natural response is to give up.

It is the role of the school administration to put teachers in a schedule that makes it possible for small groups of struggling students to get additional help. You can skip this step if you want to, but RTI will not be implemented at your school until you do it.

Conclusion

Will RTI happen at the same pace at every school? No. But there are specific things that you can do at your school to make it happen faster.

By following the four steps outlined above, you put your teachers in the best position possible to have a successful RTI implementation.

Appendix Three

RTI Professional Development

There is no doubt that the success of your school's RTI implementation will rest in the hands of the teachers. I can also assure you that the professional development that you provide for your teachers will determine their level of participation.

It is essential that you provide professional development in the area of RTI that is organized, well-planned, and sequenced correctly. The following plan for professional development plan is not the fastest, easiest, or cheapest. It is, however, the most effective way that I know to get a staff to "buy in" to the process of implementing Response to Intervention at your school.

Introduction

How you introduce your staff to RTI is one of the biggest determining factors in the success of your implementation. Teachers will make an early judgment about whether this program is worth their time and dedication. Once they make this decision, it will be very difficult to change.

There are certain attributes that are often associated with RTI when it is introduced poorly. Those attributes include:

- Complicated
- Confusing

- Difficult
- Lots of paperwork
- More difficult than what we currently do
- Time consuming

There are certain attributes that should be associated with RTI when it is introduced correctly. These attributes include:

- Simple
- Easy
- Makes sense
- Helps kids better than what we currently do
- Communicates better to parents
- Do-able

There is a big difference between the two lists. That is why the right introduction makes all of the difference.

I have recorded my simple explanation of RTI. You can hear it for free at www.totalRTI.com by clicking on the "resources" button and entering the password "audio."

If you don't think you can introduce RTI to your staff in a clear and concise way, you can simply purchase the DVD of my presentation. It lasts just 45 minutes and is filmed in high definition so you can project it on a screen for your full staff to watch together.

But I do not believe that I am the only one who can do this. If you choose to do the introduction yourself, make sure you choose someone who is knowledgeable about RTI, has experience at the grade level that the teachers teach, and can answer questions in front of a group.

Affirmation

The next three steps in the RTI Professional Development Plan are all about affirmation. We need to affirm that teachers are already doing most of RTI in their classrooms.

Three specific areas you want to offer affirmation to your teachers:

1. Affirm their use of Universal Screeners

   Your school has large amounts of performance data on your students. Teachers can use this data before the students even show up on the first day to identify which students need closer monitoring. Remember, the only purpose of a universal screening tool is to identify which students will need closer monitoring during the school year. Your teachers probably already do this, and you should affirm it!

2. Affirm their large group full-class instruction

   Tier One of RTI is full-class instruction. Most teachers that I know already stand up and teach their class. Affirm it! Make sure you are providing your teachers with a research-validated core curriculum, and when they teach it, affirm that they are doing an essential step in the RTI process.

3. Affirm the Fidelity Check of full-class instruction

> RTI requires that we observe teachers teaching to make sure they are delivering the curriculum correctly. Most schools that I visit are already doing this. Most teachers are observed during the school year by either an administrator or a colleague. Affirm this, and make sure you are recording these observations.

We are now three steps into the RTI process, and the teachers have not been asked to do anything new or different. That is why this model of RTI is described as simple, easy, and do-able.

The First Roadblock: Progress Monitoring

The first and most difficult part of implementing RTI at a school is getting teachers to use data.

The idea of regular progress monitoring of students on a single skill is not something they currently do, and it is not something they are trained to do.

MOST of your professional development in RTI during the first year of implementation needs to be in this area.

Teachers need to be trained and equipped to regularly monitor the progress of their students.

More specifically, the steps they should learn include:

> ✓ Identifying the skill they want to measure
> ✓ Choosing a tool to measure the skill

- ✓ Recording the results from the measurement
- ✓ Making a decision on effectiveness of instruction based on this data

You will need to dedicate a great deal of professional development time to this specific area, but it is worth it. RTI will not be successfully implemented in your school until teachers can do this.

One book that has been a valuable resource in helping teachers learn this skill is *The ABC's of CBM* by Michelle Hosp and friends. It sits on my desk and is a great resource.

The Second Roadblock: Small Group Interventions

There will be a small group of students who are not successful even after receiving instruction in class. RTI requires that these students receive a more intensive small group intervention or small group instruction.

The problem: Many teachers do not know how to find, where to find, or when to implement these interventions.

The solution: Professional development that is very subject-specific. This is definitely NOT when you should have your music teachers working with your math teachers.

At the elementary level, tackle one subject at a time.

At the secondary level, have teachers work in departments by subject area.

Start by having the teachers identify the most common areas where students are unsuccessful. Work together in groups to find and document interventions that work when students struggle in this area.

These small group interventions will often be purchased programs. Depending on how and when they are implemented, it may also require additional personnel to be provided to do the implementation. Computer-aided instruction is often part of this solution.

You will also need to provide time in the schedule for small group interventions. This is not really a professional development issue, unless you are going to work collaboratively to develop this new schedule.

When teachers are locked into a rigid schedule with no time to offer students extra instruction, they feel helpless and powerless. In this situation, the natural response is to give up.

It is the role of the school administration to put teachers in a schedule that makes it possible for small groups of struggling students to get additional help. You can skip this step if you want to, but RTI will not be implemented at your school until you do it.

Past the Roadblocks...

Once you overcome these two hurdles, you are home free and helping kids!

Most of the remaining steps of the process have been covered during Tier One.

The Fidelity Check of the small group intervention is to have another adult watch the instruction to see if it is being delivered correctly. Be sure to document this observation in writing.

The Progress Monitoring during the small group intervention is similar to the progress monitoring during Tier One. It is done with all students receiving the small group instruction.

At the end of this process, there may be an eligibility process to determine the student's eligibility for special education services. If this is the case, make sure that you teach this process to your staff and let them know what data they will be expected to present at these meetings.

A Word about Paperwork

If I hear one negative comment about RTI more than others, it is: "The paperwork is overwhelming!"

You need to change this. You need to simplify the paperwork involved.

It is possible to take a student through most of the RTI process with just seven pieces of paper.

What's the first piece of paperwork? The first piece of paperwork was the Universal Screening results.

What's the second piece of paperwork? That's the full-class intervention – what curriculum was being taught.

What's the third piece of paperwork? It's the Fidelity Check – the written documentation of the full-class intervention observation.

The fourth piece of paperwork is the graph from the progress monitoring during Tier One.

And the fifth piece of paperwork is the small-group intervention and the Fidelity Check of that small-group intervention.

The sixth piece of paper is the progress monitoring graph from the small group intervention.

What's the seventh piece of paper? Well, there are really only six, but I figure you will come up with some other hoop to jump through, so I just wanted to give you some wiggle room to do that.

People often say, "How do you not get overwhelmed with the paperwork that comes with RTI?"

Well, you don't get overwhelmed by creating a simple system of managing paperwork. In my model of RTI, I am able to take a student from 'non-identified' through 'ready for identification for special education' in less than seven pieces of paper. You don't get overwhelmed with paperwork because you have a limited number of students that you're doing this with, and it's just a few pieces of paper for each student.

Now, I know many of you are struggling with Response to Intervention right now, because you're in systems that require piles and piles of paper. Those systems are designed for failure.

Until you are serious about simplifying the RTI process, it is not going to be implemented fully at your school, because teachers simply will not fully embrace a system that creates so much paperwork that it is unmanageable.

Conclusion

As you can see from this plan, there are three main areas of focus in this Professional Development Plan:

An introduction that is simple

Teach progress monitoring to your teachers

Help selecting and implementing small group interventions

If you do these three things well and limit the paperwork burden, you are well on your way to a successful implementation of Response to Intervention at your school!

Appendix Four

Examples of Progress Monitoring Tools by Specific Area

Finding effective universal screening tools and progress monitoring tools can be a challenging task. The list below is not intended to be a complete list. Instead, it is offered as a list of examples to get you started in your search.

Oral Reading Fluency
DIBELS

Early Literacy
AIMSweb
STAR

Early Numeracy
AIMSweb

Initial Sound Fluency
DIBELS
Vital Indicators of Progress (VIP)

Letter Naming Fluency
Vital Indicators of Progress (VIP)

Math
Accelerated Math and Reader
AIMSweb
Monitoring Basic Skills Progress (MBSP)
PASeries
STAR
Yearly Progress Pro

Maze
AIMSweb
EdCheckup

Nonsense Word Fluency
DIBELS
Vital Indicators of Progress (VIP)

Phoneme Segmentation
Vital Indicators of Progress (VIP)

Phonemic
DIBELS

Phonemic Decode Efficiency
Test of Word Reading Efficiency (TOWRE)

Reading
Accelerated Math and Reader
AIMSweb
EdCheckup
Monitoring Basic Skills Progress (MBSP)
PASeries
STAR

Test of Silent Word Reading Fluency (TOSWRF)
Yearly Progress Pro

Reading Fluency
iSTEEP (System to Enhance Educational Performance)

Retell Fluency
DIBELS

Segmentation Fluency
DIBELS

Sight Word Efficiency
Test of Word Reading Efficiency (TOWRE)

Spelling
AIMSweb

Word Use Fluency
DIBELS

Written Expression
AIMSweb

Find additional information and websites for many of these tools at:

http://www.studentprogress.org/

Examples of Interventions by Area

Finding effective interventions targeted to a specific deficiency is one of the most challenging parts of implementing RTI. The list below is not intended to be a complete list of interventions. Instead, it is offered as a list of examples to get you started in your search.

Beginning Reading Interventions:
Reading Recovery®
Accelerated Reader/Reading Renaissance
Classwide Peer Tutoring©
Little Books
Success for All
95% Group

Reading Fluency Interventions:
Reading Recovery®
Ladders to Literacy
95% Group
Corrective Reading
Fluency Formula™
Kaplan SpellRead

Secondary Literacy & Writing:
SOLO Literacy Suite

Reading Comprehension Interventions:
Kaplan SpellRead
Early Intervention in Reading (EIR)®
Start Making a Reader Today® (SMART®)
Reading Recovery®

Peer-Assisted Learning Strategies (PALS)©
Accelerated Reader/Reading Renaissance
Failure Free Reading
Read 180

Elementary Mathematics:
Math Facts Fluency
Everyday Mathematics
Building Blocks for Math (SRA Real Math)
Pre-K Mathematics

Middle School and High School Math:
Skillstutor Math
Study Island
The Expert Mathematician
Cognitive Tutor® Algebra I
I CAN Learn® Pre-Algebra and Algebra

Behavior:
Personal Development
Discipline with Purpose
Positive Action
Too Good For Violence (TGFV)
Connect with Kids
Too Good for Drugs™ (TGFD)

Academic Achievement:
Lessons in Character
Positive Action

Find additional information and websites for many of these tools at the "What Works Clearinghouse" website.

Appendix Five

Now, It's Your Turn

I hope that this book and the suggestions from other educational professionals who are implementing RTI have given you a greater depth of understanding of what RTI is and how you can integrate it into your classroom.

To that end, I've included this last section to help you assess your school's Response to Intervention progress. By answering the questions on the following pages, I also hope you can identify strategies which you can use in implementing RTI. Your answers will also help you locate resources which are available to you in your school.

I encourage you to use creativity and teamwork as you develop your school's RTI program. Remember, RTI works best when everyone cooperates.

Successful Response to Intervention benefits everyone!

What "Universal Screenings" does your school currently have in place?

What parts of your curriculum are
scientifically validated? Which are not?

What are ways you monitor and record student progress?

When could you make time during the day to deliver Tier 2 small group interventions?

What scientifically validated small group interventions do you have for students when your full-class instruction does not work?

What is your plan for being observed for fidelity? How will you record this observation?

What is your plan for communicating the progress of students to their parents?

If a Tier 2 small group intervention does not work, what is the next decision-making process?

What additional personnel are available at your school to help with Tier 2 small group intervention and progress monitoring?

What barriers does your school have to successful implementation of RTI? How can you overcome those barriers?

PAT QUINN
"The RTI Guy!"

Pat Quinn has spent his entire career helping struggling students become successful in school. As a teacher, author, and nationally recognized keynote speaker, he has changed thousands of lives through his insightful message. Pat Quinn helps educators around the country improve their teaching, renew their passion, and lengthen their careers as he speaks about closing the achievement gap and meeting the needs of all students.

Mr. Quinn is the author of twelve books on meeting the individual needs of students, including *Designing an Alternative Curriculum* and the bestselling *Changing Lives*. He has taught undergraduate courses for Lakeland College and graduate courses at Alverno College. He is the former editor of the educational newsletter *The Unconventional Teacher*.

To subscribe to Pat Quinn's RTI newsletter, visit:

www.TotalRTI.com

Email Pat Quinn at: pat@betterteachingonline.com